A
TEAM
MEMBER'S
GUIDE
TO
PROJECT
MANAGEMENT

A
TEAM
MEMBER'S
GUIDE
TO
PROJECT
MANAGEMENT

The Fundaments of Project and Program Management

Richard Champney, PMP, *and*
Robert Kubacki, J.D., M.P.A.

Archway Publishing books may be ordered through booksellers or by contacting:

Archway Publishing
1663 Liberty Drive
Bloomington, IN 47403
www.archwaypublishing.com
1 (888) 242-5904

Because of the dynamic nature of the Internet, any web addresses or links contained in this book may have changed since publication and may no longer be valid. The views expressed in this work are solely those of the author and do not necessarily reflect the views of the publisher, and the publisher hereby disclaims any responsibility for them.

Any people depicted in stock imagery provided by Thinkstock are models, and such images are being used for illustrative purposes only. Certain stock imagery © Thinkstock.

ISBN: 978-1-4808-5077-4 (sc)
ISBN: 978-1-4808-5078-1 (e)

Library of Congress Control Number: 2017951781

Print information available on the last page.

Archway Publishing rev. date: 02/23/2018

To Pierrette and Susan.

TABLE OF CONTENTS

ACKNOWLEDGMENTS

This book would not have been possible without the support our spouses, friends, and colleagues. Our many thanks to everyone who took time out of their busy days to read our many drafts, listen to our struggles to simplify our story, provide such valuable feedback, and many times, provide the encouragement to move forward.

Molly Bissell, CJ Bourn, Joe Gifford, Mike Green, Bob Kelly, Bill Kennedy, Gary Olliffe, Joe Raynus, Rob Rudd, Dean Seinbach, and those we may have missed—thanks for your encouragement, edits, criticisms, and excellent suggestions.

ABOUT THIS BOOK

Several years ago, a US university discovered that after graduation, many of their PhD and graduate students struggled in making the transition from an academic to business environment.

To help in that transition they asked us to provide a lecture on project management to their post-graduate students. Their interest was high and their questions insightful. As our workshop material evolved and taking into consideration our own experience as project managers and team members, we realized that team members' interests and perspectives were vastly different from that of their project managers.

A project team member's success and a project's success depends on a balanced combination of the "hard" skills of methods and procedures of project management and the interpersonal or "soft" skills of relationship building and communication.

This book is not about how to be a project manager or program manager. This is a book for people who find themselves working on a project using project management tools.

Richard the engineer and Robert the conflict management professional bring backgrounds that reflect those hard and soft skill areas. Richard has managed engineering organizations and project teams that have spanned the globe in commercial and military product development. Robert's work as legal counsel to state agencies and nonprofit organizations includes the roles of mediator, conflict coach, public administrator and adjunct faculty teaching courses in conflict resolution, communication, management and business.

So please join us as we explore what it means to be a team member and why having a rudimentary knowledge of the anatomy of a project is so important to helping every team member gain control, manage change, and reduce the chaos and confusion often found with so many projects.

PART I
A PROJECT

CHAPTER 1

PROJECT BASICS

You recently joined a project team. The meeting format and topics may seem a bit odd, the terminology is sometimes cryptic, and priorities seem mixed up. What is this all about?

Let's start with two concepts common to all projects.

First, by definition, a project has a beginning, middle, and end. If it doesn't have that, you are not working on a project.

Second, a project is focused on three topics called the "iron triangle." This triangle is composed of three legs:

1. Time   How long it will take?
2. Cost   How much money is required?
3. Scope   What needs to be produced?

Mathematics tells us if one leg of a triangle changes, something else in the triangle must change to maintain the triangle. It is the same with the iron triangle. If one leg of the iron triangle changes, something else in your project plan must change.

The Iron Triangle

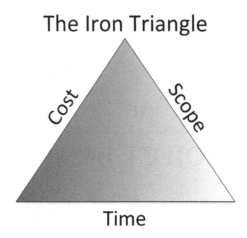

Time

That's it! Understand these two concepts and you understand the basics of project management.

With an understanding of the definitions of these two concepts, activities such as cooking a meal or buying groceries are projects. Every day you and countless others manage and accomplish simple projects on a regular basis. With this awareness, it may surprise you that you possess more project management experience and skill than you thought you had.

We are usually quite successful managing our everyday activities. This makes you a project manager with a great track record and lots of expertise. Well, that is true until you ask someone to help you on your project.

For example, getting groceries is a simple project you do quite well when you do it all by yourself. Did you ever ask somebody to get groceries for you?

A wife asks her husband, "Could you please go shopping for me and buy one carton of milk, and if they have eggs, get six!" A short time later the husband comes back with six cartons of milk. The wife asks him, "Why did you buy six cartons of milk?"

He replies, "They had eggs."

Has something similar ever happened to you? The husband and wife misunderstood each other, and the outcome was not what each expected. If communication for as something as simple as grocery shopping can become confused, imagine how easy it is for a project covering many departments, spanning cultures around the world and areas of expertise, can lead to misunderstanding and conflicts

Success depends on more than forms and reports. It relies upon clear and transparent communication.

Communication Basics

When two or more people communicate in everyday conversation, it is easy to misinterpret what the other means. When communicating with a number of people about a project's tasks or deliverables, the chance for misinterpretation and hurt feelings increases exponentially.

The root cause of most project failures is a breakdown in communication.

To be successful, communication must be a two-way exchange of information and shared meaning of words. Unless it is, the terminology used in project team meetings is sometimes perplexing.

To understand the importance of communication to a project team, we created the "silk triangle" as an easy way to recognize and keep track of the types of interpersonal communications that are essential to the successful functioning of any project team.

The silk triangle is composed of three legs:

1. Communicate   Was the communication understood?
2. Relate   How well do we know each other?
3. Debate   Can we disagree and move on?

From experience, we know that the silk triangle is as equally important to project success as the hard iron triangle.

The silk triangle, like the iron triangle, is a concept that states a simple truth. If one leg of the triangle changes, something else must change. If they don't, then the resulting imbalance is likely to undermine the project's success. This impediment to a project's success is fueled by misunderstandings, slights to members' egos, passive-aggressive behavior, and team members looking out for their own interests.

As you read our story about a family's fence-building project, keep in mind the iron and silk triangles

Like a project, our story has a beginning, a middle, and an end. It recounts how siblings who decide to build a fence to decorate the front yard of their parents' home manage that project. They will have set parameters for their iron triangle (a budget, a schedule, and a product), and test the strength of their silk triangle (communicate, relate, debate). Just like any project team, these siblings must understand the budget, project schedule, and project scope for constructing a fence. Their shared understanding of the iron triangle will depend on how well they manage their silk triangle. Regardless of how well they do that, like all projects, a few surprises await them.

Our fence story intends to provide an answer to the statement we sometimes run into from project team members: "This project management stuff doesn't apply to me or my project." Yes, it does. Maybe your team doesn't use written forms, and maybe you don't have formal meetings with notes and action items, but plans are made, decisions are applied, and work is done in a fairly predictable manner.

As projects get more complex and more people join the team, project managers turn those discussions and thoughts into documents that employ a variety of tools we use to improve communications, decision-making, and planning. The purpose of these tools is to make everyone's life easier and to achieve success.

CHAPTER 2

INITIATE PROJECT
(FORM A PLAN)

A Saturday-evening lawn party is in full swing. Children, grandchildren, and friends are all gathered to celebrate Walter and Mary's fiftieth wedding anniversary. Everyone is admiring the newly installed fence in the front yard. After being away on a day trip, Walter and Mary arrived home to find a beautiful fence bordering their front yard. Everyone on the project team was pleased that the fence was the perfect surprise gift. They also congratulated themselves that the project had gone so well.

How did this project have such a wonderful outcome? Let's find out.

Sisters Susan and Audrey met at their favorite downtown coffee shop every Saturday morning before their weekly grocery shopping.

They were discussing their mom and dad's upcoming wedding anniversary and wondering, what should they do to make it a special occasion?

Susan had a great idea. "Let's send Mom and Dad on a dream vacation to a tropical island. All the brothers and sisters can contribute equally to make this a dream vacation for Mom and Dad.'"

Audrey wasn't so sure. She said, "You know ever since Dad hurt his back, he hasn't been interested in traveling."

Susan replied, "Sure, but maybe he'll be better by then. It really would be a way for the whole family to say thanks for all the sacrifices they made to raise a family of six children who are now living on their own and doing well."

Audrey was concerned about the cost. "As you know, our younger brother Travis is starting his new business, and contributing money for a vacation fund would be really tough for him. Why don't we try something different?"

"Maybe a new refrigerator?" Susan suggested. They both quickly agreed that wasn't something Mom and Dad would enjoy.

Susan had another idea. "Well, Dad and Mom have always said how nice their house would look with a decorative fence in the front yard. Dad can't install it with his bad back. Maybe we could do something like that."

Now Audrey was excited. "Sure, we could form a work team, and all of us could build the fence on a day when Mom and Dad are out of the house and surprise them with a new fence when they return! It wouldn't cost as much as a trip to the tropics. It would be a lot of fun having all of us working together, including our friends and extended family. And then we can have everyone there for a surprise lawn party for Mom and Dad when they return."

Susan agreed.

Now they had an idea for a project that had a beginning, a middle and an end.

That evening Susan and Audrey started calling their brothers and sisters.

CHAPTER 3

BUILDING A TEAM

Reactions to their idea were mixed.

Brothers David and Alex and sister Jenna were excited and thought it was a great idea. They were happy to contribute time and money. They volunteered their spouses and kids to help out. Travis had some reservations. Actually, his concerns were quite valid. What kind of fence did they have in mind? Did Mom and Dad really want a decorative fence or a privacy fence? Did everyone agree to spend lots of money on maintenance-free materials, or did they want to save money using less costly wood that Travis would likely wind up painting every few years? And how could they do all that work in a single day— dig holes, paint boards, and build a fence?

With all of these questions and options to sort out, building a fence was becoming more complex by the minute. It soon became obvious that one of them had to lead this effort if they were to pull it off.

After much discussion, everyone agreed that Alex should to take the lead. She was available, and she had a real talent for organizing people and getting things done.

CHAPTER 4

MAKING A PLAN

Alex soon discovered a lot of issues. After speaking with her family and friends, she discovered as many questions as answers. To manage this, she created an issues list that categorized general topics of the scope that had to be resolved before the project could begin. Issues such as: How would they dig holes that wouldn't tear up the yard yet dig fast enough to be completed in a day? Could they afford expensive materials that never needed painting, or would they have to use less-expensive wood that required annual maintenance? How would they sort out all the work with the people available? Using an *issues list,* Alex laid out each issue, who had responsibility for getting the answer, when was the answer due, and what was the final resolution for each one.

Mom and Dad's Fence			
Issues List			
Description	Owner	Answer Due	Resolution
Can we afford a maintenance-free plastic fence, or do we paint wood?	Alex	Thursday	Paint wood; plastic exceeds our budget
How do we get Mom and Dad out of the house when we are there building the fence?	Susan & Audrey	Wednesday	Their best friends will take them to the mountains for the day.
Who's going to organize and host the backyard party at 5:00 p.m. after the fence is built?	Susan & Audrey	Wednesday	Susan, Audrey, Patti, and Bruce will organize the party and not work on the fence project.

As Alex and her project team resolved those issues, it became obvious to everyone what had to be done within the agreed-upon budget and in a realistic timeframe.

After creating with her siblings an issues list, Alex instinctively knew that the next step was to turn her attention to a task list. Like a grocery shopping list, her task list would simply define what had to be done when and by whom.

Mom and Dad's Fence Task List		
Task	Owner	Due Date
Rent posthole digger	Jenna	1 week before
Buy boards, nails, and paint	Audrey	1 days before
Compile hammers, saws, shovels, tarps, etc.	Vanessa	2 days before
Invitations	Susan & Audrey	3 weeks before
Determine budget and gather donations from brothers and sisters	Susan & Audrey	3 weeks before

Alex quickly recognized that her task list was more complicated than she originally thought it would be. Some tasks couldn't start until other actions were underway or completed. This meant she had to make sure each task was listed. By doing so, the interdependence of various tasks became apparent to all of the sibling project team members. Alex captured the interdependence of critical tasks graphically by making a *Gantt chart*. This is a project management tool that plots out the amount of time each task requires and the order in which it is performed.

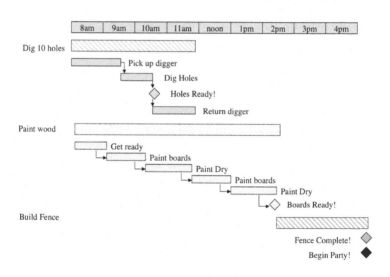

Like with the issues and task lists, the siblings discussed a variety ways to sequence the various activities. Some suggested that the posthole diggers could sleep late and start digging holes after lunch (they would still be done before the paint was dry), but the team decided that an early-morning start to hole digging would let them save money by returning the posthole digger back to the rental center early enough to pay for only a half-day rental.

We will skip the details of the numerous phone calls and coffee shop meetings that Alex arranged and everyone participated in to resolve a variety of simple and sometimes difficult issues, including who would do which tasks and when. These meetings were supplemented with e-mails, texts, and even social media. At times one sibling or another thought they heard one thing or everyone agreed with the idea, only to learn they had misunderstood what was said. Eventually, with Alex's guidance, the siblings developed a team mentality, and found ways to argue without bruising feelings or egos. The most general items of their project plan were captured in the Gantt chart. Their plan satisfied everyone's concerns, and everyone was on the same page as what had to be done and which team (hole-digger team, wood-painting team, and fence-building team) would do it by when.

CHAPTER 5

RECOGNIZING RISK

From experience with her own everyday projects, Alex knew that it doesn't matter how well a plan is thought through, there is always risk that may or may not be within the control of the project team. Alex knew she had to consider, among other things: What if it rains? What if somebody gets sick? What if Mom and Dad won't leave the house on the day we are building the fence?

Alex knew that the solution to this challenge was to build a *risk register* early in the planning stage. She understood that capturing those risks early enough in the project planning phase had a direct influence on building a robust plan for the project's budget, schedule, and scope of work. As a communication tool, it would help lower the volume of her siblings who inclined to blame when something went wrong.

Alex soon discovered that there are three basic issues with any risk register; probability (how likely is that risk going to actually happen?), impact (if the risk becomes true, is it a big deal or trivial?), and reaction (what, if anything, are we going to do to mitigate that risk?).

Mom and Dad's Fence Risk Register					
Description	Probability	Impact	Owner	Answer Due	Mitigation
We can't find a Saturday where everyone can participate.	low	high	Susan & Audrey	6 weeks before	If we can't find a Saturday where everyone can participate, we will cancel the fence project and do something different for an anniversary gift.
What if it rains?	medium	low	Alex	3 days before	Rent a lawn tent to keep rain off painters and later host the party under the tent.
What if Mom and Dad won't go to the mountains or leave for the day until 5:00 p.m.?	low	low	Susan & Audrey	1 day before	We will tell Mom and Dad and not have this a surprise.

After completing the risk register, Alex was a bit alarmed that if certain risks occurred, the entire project would come to a halt. For these big risks, Alex decided to fashion a plan B. For example, if it looked like it might rain, Alex would rent large tents to keep much of the work team and the evening partygoers dry. She knew she didn't have to make that decision (and spend that money) until a few days before when the weather forecast was the most reliable. She did put a hold on tent just in case. Alex was smart enough to know that even decisions must be scheduled in a well-managed project.

CHAPTER 6

LET'S GET STARTED!

Six chapters into our story and Alex and her sibling project team has yet to dig a hole or paint a board.

For some time, Travis had been upset with Alex. Her insisting on writing up lists, charts, and graphs were from Travis's perspective a big waste of time and energy. Travis thought Alex spent more time chatting at the coffee shop with her brothers and sisters than actually working on getting the fence built. For all the time taken up with talking, they could have built two fences! Travis couldn't understand why getting started was being delayed. He knew that all they had to do was buy some boards and paint them, reserve a posthole digger at the rental store, and invite everyone to show up on Saturday.

Like many disgruntled project team members, Travis didn't keep his criticisms to himself. He let anyone who would listen know that he didn't like the way Alex was running the project. Susan and Audrey finally had to meet alone with Travis and remind him that this was their idea, everyone agreed to it, and everyone agreed to let Alex lead the project. They made it very clear to Travis that it was too late to start over again or follow a different course. If he wanted to remain on the project, he had to stop complaining about how Alex was managing the project. They liked the fact that Alex asked for their suggestions and had built a plan that made sense. They suggested that maybe Travis ought to read his e-mails from Alex. Those charts and lists captured every team member's issues and answered all their questions, including the ones Travis asked. After that chat with his sisters, Travis reluctantly agreed to follow the plan Alex and the team had put together with Alex's efforts and to stop his complaining.

Finally, the big day arrived. Audrey used her truck to pick up all the necessary wood, paint, and nails on Friday night. Saturday morning Jenna picked up the posthole digger. Walter and Mary's best friends agreed to take them away for a day trip.

CHAPTER 7

SATURDAY MORNING

Saturday's forecast called for a sunny and warm day. Everyone showed up early because Alex sent out several reminders about the start time. Everyone pitched in to organize the materials for the day ahead. Jenna showed up a bit late with the posthole digger due to a long line at the rental center, but everything remained on schedule.

After finishing their coffees and catching up on the latest news, the painters started painting and the hole diggers started on time right to the Gannt chart's schedule.

Renting the hole digger was a great idea. David and Travis were digging holes at a fantastic pace, and within an hour, they had eight of the ten holes dug. Travis was in a good mood and started to tease the painters, "Hurry up, we are eighty percent finished with the postholes. You won't have your fence boards ready in time!"

They started to dig the ninth hole when they hit the rock. It was a really big rock. How big? It was as wide as a car. There wasn't any way they would be able to dig around it or remove it. The hole digging came to a halt.

This was a serious problem. If they didn't dig a hole deep enough to install the fence post, they couldn't complete the fence in time.

CHAPTER 8

THE ROCK (A PROJECT SURPRISE)

For Alex and her siblings, hitting a rock, let alone one as large as this one, came as a big surprise. The fact that it threatened their chances of building the fence in one day caught them completely off guard. Even though they created a comprehensive task list, and a risk register with a mitigation plan for all of the listed risks, no one had foreseen rocks, let alone a rock this big in the very place where the fence posts had to be dug.

Although earlier Travis had confidently declared that the hole digging was 80 percent complete, hole digging was no longer 80 percent complete. Alex and her project team had an unexpected problem to solve and a lot more work ahead of them

Soon enough the shouting began as well as assigning blame. The painters all stopped painting and came over to see what was going on. Everyone chimed in with ideas about what to do.

Travis said to Alex, "Why didn't you think we might hit a rock and put it on the risk list?"

Alex replied, "Let's fix this problem and not waste our time on what should have been done."

Alex became aware that the painters had stopped painting and needed to get back to work as any delays in painting would delay the completion of the project. With painters back on task, Alex could focus on exploring options, selecting the best option, and carrying out a plan of action. Her first step was to solicit ideas.

Ideas were abundant. Use dynamite and blow up the rock; cut the post shorter and make braces to keep it upright; just give up and make a eight-post fence; and on and on the ideas flew.

Many of the ideas had merit. However, choosing the best solution was tough as there were tradeoffs with each idea. Dynamite needed special permits and specialists, meaning days if not weeks to complete the holes. Adding braces would be quick and easy but also ugly. Other ideas were weighed against the iron triangle parameters of scope, schedule, and cost. Because Alex had established a protocol for debating and relating as a team, the communication among those suggesting ideas was constructive and courteous. One team member suggested that they cut the post shorter and bolt it to the rock, and everyone agreed this was the best idea. Susan's husband was a contractor and had special drills and adhesives to cut holes and set bolts in concrete that also would work on this rock.

Alex knew they were now deviating from the original plan, but it was critical for the project's success that they do so. It took a few hours to get the tools from Susan's house, drill the holes, and set the bolts. The final two posts were installed with plenty of time to spare before the final coat of paint had dried.

CHAPTER 9

FINISHING UP

The rest of the project went smoothly. The posts were all set, the painted boards were nailed to the posts, postholes were filled in, and the lawn was raked and cleaned. There was no sign that the fence had been built in one day. With enough time to spare, everyone got ready for the fantastic party Audrey, Susan, Jenna, and David had put together.

When Walter and Mary arrived home with their friends, everyone on cue came out from their hiding places and yelled, "Happy anniversary." Walter and Mary couldn't believe all their family and friends were there, and they couldn't believe that they had a new fence in front of their house.

PART II

REVIEWING THE STORY AS A MANAGED PROJECT

So let's review our story from the perspective of a project member and the siblings project team performance. Your project has much in common with our fence project. Building a fence in a day may much simpler than the project you are working on. However, it is still a project, and there are components common to your project—no matter how large or small, no matter how complex or basic.

Sponsors

Every project has a sponsor. Audrey and Susan are the sponsors in this story. They spent a good deal of time and energy determining the best gift to their parents. They balanced the tradeoffs between gift ideas of expense paid trips, appliances, or extravagant parties. Their project was defined by their family's wishes and restrictions in time, money, and the scope of work they wanted to accomplish.

Your sponsor *is not your customer!* This is a misunderstanding many project team members have and it can result in confusion and costly mistakes. Customers can be internal to your company, an entity contracting with your business, or a market composed of millions of buyers. Be sure to understand the difference between the sponsor (who defines the project) and the customer (who uses the product).

Sponsors could be the board of directors, your boss, or someone else who provides the definition and resources to make a project happen.

It is vital that you understand who is your project's sponsor and what exactly he or she wants. For example, your sponsor may want a new consumer product created. He or she will decide if it is intended to be a high-volume and low-cost product that sells in the millions or a premium performance item with limited appeal at its high cost. Both ideas could be very successful. But it is the sponsor that defines the project and the resulting customers it will serve.

As the conversation between Audrey and Susan demonstrates, the project may go through several iterations as the sponsors consider market research, competitive analysis, or limited company budgets to create a project that aligns with company goals and brings the highest probability of success.

Team Members

Some teams are comprised of team members who volunteer or are assigned from within or from different departments. If you work with someone on the team, do your best to get to know your teammates and their specific project assignment. By relating with other team members, you can learn a lot from them, share work, avoid duplication of effort, and avoid misunderstandings when you communicate or argue with them about some aspect of the project.

In our story, Travis questioned the sponsor's plan. This is common with any project as new people join the team and try their best to understand the goals and constraints they are working under. Not everyone takes in or processes information in the same way. Some are visual learners, others auditory, and others need hands-on activity to make sense of and to accomplish instructions. Communication is important throughout the life of a project. It is the only way to quickly get all the team members up to speed on the sponsor's objectives.

When a new member joins a team, you and everyone else on the team is responsible for bringing that person up to date and more importantly familiarizing him or her with how the team functions. You might want to consider building a project book. This is a quick guide for people joining the project team after it begins or for people who may not be engaged for long periods of time. This can be a folder on a shared computer drive or a binder with documents. Its purpose is to get new team members up to speed on objectives, who's doing what (who do you see) for deliverables and ownership, decisions made so far, progress to date, and the plan ahead.

Project Planning

> Give me six hours to chop down a tree and I will
> spend the first four sharpening the ax.
>
> —Abraham Lincoln

Everyone agrees that good preparation helps with success. We find this topic to be one of the most frustrating and confusing ones for many people. In our story, Travis is a team member who is action oriented; let's just get started and we can work it out as we go along. At the other extreme is the micro-planner who wastes time and money generating reams of documents that nobody reads and whose documents quickly become obsolete as rocks get discovered and require a change in plans.

If you don't plan and track your work, it is difficult if not impossible to know if you will meet the goals of the iron triangle until you are all done. If you hit a rock, it is too late to mitigate. If the silk triangle's factors are ignored, when a team hits its rock, it has no tried and true mechanisms for how that team can move quickly from blame, criticism, and gossiping to collaborative problem solving.

But there is no one-size-fits-all solution for this issue. Each project must be planned appropriately to the project demands. Building a new airplane in which hundreds of people will trust their lives requires a level of detail, documentation, and risk management far in excess of anything expected for a low-cost table lamp. Yet an airplane or a table lamp both require an appropriate level of documentation and regulatory compliance to assure the product does not injure anyone.

One last consideration—a plan that incorporates or at the very least openly acknowledge team members' experience, training, insight, cultural (ethnic, professional, etc.) perspectives, and opinions is much stronger than a plan that does not. Inviting diverse opinions can be painful and disruptive or a dynamic and rewarding experience that produces a host of solutions and bonds a project team together. When a project manager solicits ideas or solutions, this doesn't mean every "great" idea will be accepted, especially if it negatively affects the constraints of the iron triangle.

If a project manager delegates a project-planning activity to you, we suggest you circulate it among some of your team members to gather feedback and suggestions to make your plan the best it can be.

Successful project planning is as much about the legs of the silk triangle (communicate, relate, and debate) as it is about the iron triangle (time, cost, and scope).

It is important to remember that having a plan and then locking it away is a waste of time. Project planning is more than checking off items on a list. As a project is underway, plans dissolve because assumptions are sometimes wrong and the plan is likely to be out of sync with everyday realities. Plans often require updates to reflect that new knowledge. As a team member, you will be asked to contribute to task lists, issues lists, risk registers, and Gantt chart updates. The level of detail, information needed, and update frequency will be determined by the type of project you have and the needs of your sponsors, customers, and project team. Your contributions of knowledge, expertise, and insights could make the difference as to whether a project succeeds or not.

Risk Management

Risk management is on our list of things that can frustrate and confuse project team members. Typically risk registers measure three topics: probability of the event occurring, the impact if it does occur, and the mitigation plan to reduce or eliminate the impact of that risk. Risk management can guide the plan forward. It is reasonable and prudent to put some money and time in reserve just to handle risks, as a few risks are likely to come true. As a useful and influential team member, you need to communicate the risks as you see them in your area of expertise; nobody understands those risks as well as you. The earlier in the project they are identified, the more likely they will not be a show stopper.

Our story has one risk identified in the risk register that can even shut down the project: not finding a weekend that fits into everyone's schedule. Knowing when to make the decision to shut down a project could be a risk scheduled into your risk register.

If you anticipate a problem might occur, capture it on the risk register. Your thoughts become visible, the team can debate how and decide if they want to prepare for such a possibility, along with what might be done if the anticipated problem occurs. This is where the communicate leg of the silk triangle comes to the fore. Unless each member hears, understands, and acknowledges receipt of a message, individual team members may quickly find themselves at cross purposes because the project plan has made a shift in direction.

Well-managed risk can keep a project moving even when it hits a rock. Useful 'what if' planning can enable a project team to sort out tasks and activities to reduce risks at the start of the project and assure budget, schedule, and scope capture risk at the beginning of your effort. When a project is in full swing, it can save time and needless arguments because what needs to occur to mitigate a program is a pre-programmed decision.

Designing a risk register requires a balance between

devoting too much time, energy and attention to finding perfect solutions for each risk and spending too little time, energy, and attention to finding workable solutions. If the middle way is not followed, it means the project team is running blind and likely to trip over the project's unforeseen big rock.

Issues List

Issues are topics that need the attention of the team. The scale and scope of any resulting activities are often determined as the issue is resolved. For example, in business determining if your company makes a part or has someone make it for you is an important issue. It is an issue whose answer is based on many topics, such as skills, resource availability, time requirements, and other business and quality requirements. Our project has an issue regarding wooden or plastic (paint-free) boards. For this family, that decision will be based on budgets. Resolution of issues impacts the legs of our iron triangle: budget, scope, and time.

Task List

Unlike issues that need answers, tasks are the answers that need to get done. You may hear of a work breakdown structure (WBS), which further details those tasks into logical grouping of topics and departments. A good task list helps everyone know what will be done by whom and when.

Future tasks may seem obvious to the team members, but taking the time to create that list avoids the simple things that are often missed ("I thought you were doing it. No, they said you were doing it!"). Sorting out tasks will often raise conflict or confusion about roles, responsibilities, and ownership of the tasks. This sorting out is to be expected and is usually accomplished with debates and arguments. When the debating is over and relationships are rebalanced, it is time to make sure relationships were not a casualty of a vigorous debate.

Every team member is responsible for communicating and doing their part to ensure that team members are working together. Ignoring any one of the legs of the silk triangle is likely to foster resentments. If left unattended, they will grow. Just when the project seems to be on track, those resentments will come back to undo all the progress that was made. The time invested up front on clearly debating and making sure everyone understands the task list will pay huge dividends on team morale and performance.

Critical Path and Slack

Critical path is a collection of the activities that define the time needed to complete a project. Any delay in one of the critical path activities will have a direct delay on the completion date for the project.

Activities not on the critical path have what is called *slack*. This means an activity can start or end with some delay and have no impact on our project schedule. If delayed too much, an activity with slack can become the new critical path. Digging postholes was a slack activity. They did not have to start in the morning; they could have started digging holes after lunch and still be finished before the paint was dry for fence assembly. Their decision to start in the morning left slack at the end of the project day rather the beginning—which is a good planning approach. When they hit the rock in the morning, they had time to resolve the surprise without delaying the overall project schedule.

Multitasking is how we live our lives and plan our projects. But if you want to know which tasks to prioritize, work on the critical path to keep the project on schedule. The critical chain project methodology states that anyone working on the critical path must not multitask but rather spend all their effort to complete on schedule or earlier to create a safety buffer (to handle any surprise ahead). You will recall that Alex told the painters to get back to painting (it was the critical path) as the rest of the team addressed the rock crisis.

Let's look at the critical path in our Gantt chart.

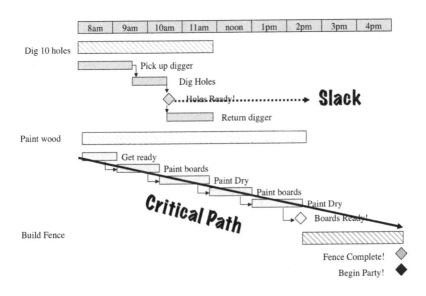

Notice that watching paint dry is on the critical path! The noise and dust of digging holes is a big deal. Even hitting a rock is a big deal ... but none of that is on the critical path. It isn't always obvious where the critical path is in your project. If it is not provided, ask. It will help you and everyone else prioritize the project's work. This is why communication is so important to ensure that all team members are moving in the same direction.

Percent Complete

As Travis discovered, determining percent complete is not an easy task. Telling your boss you are 80 percent complete, only to change it the next day to a value less than 80 percent is not good for your credibility. The confusion rises with the metric you use. In other words, which leg or legs of the iron triangle are you using? Travis was correct that 80 percent of the holes were dug when he reported progress on that scope of work. Unfortunately, that is not 80 percent of the time, nor is it 80 percent of the cost. If the metrics being used for reporting progress are communicated effectively and understood, then feedback reports from team members will be credible and understood.

If you work on projects with progress payments, those payments are often tied to percent completion. A method often used by the US government for contractor accomplishment payments is earned value management (EVM). If you use EVM, you know that it can be complex in its planning and measurement because it does consider the three legs of the iron triangle. EVM is beyond the scope of this book. There are many fine books and classes available that provide training and tools for EVM users. Let us just summarize by saying that measuring progress is not trivial, and when you do, make sure everyone understands the metrics you are using.

PART III

THE PROJECT
VARIABLES LOOP

The purpose of our story and this preceding review is to provide you with additional thoughts and insights into making your projects less stressful and more successful. With all projects, the project variables loop exists. The variables listed and discussed below are aspects that provide contour and contrast to any project plan.

Communication

The importance of communication cannot be overemphasized. It is critical as it is every team member's responsibility, not just the project manager's. Small projects with a small team may communicate over morning coffee or passing in the hallways. The danger is that not everyone on the team may be there or informed about what transpired during that informal conversation with formal consequences. To keep everyone up to date and in sync, assigning someone to be the team communication point person is a way to make sure everyone is informed. This can be as simple as a weekly e-mail updating all team members about project status as well as any changes or decisions affecting the project.

Large projects spanning time zones and even countries will need to employ more formal communication methods. Expect regular scheduled meetings and meeting minutes. Expect you'll be using the task list, risk register, issues list, Gantt chart, budget reports, and such. Know what they are and how you can contribute to them. They are all communication tools in addition to being project management tools.

Regardless of the size of a project or the project team or distance and time zones, social talk is as important as project talk. Getting to know your team members is a low-cost way to improve project success. When you discover shared interests, ways of communicating, or perspectives, you are no longer a member of a team; you are a team member. Each team builds its own way of doing things, its own culture so to speak. The more familiar team members become with each other, the more trust will follow. It is trust that holds a team together when differences of opinions lead to disagreements and conflict. It is easier to ascribe good intent to someone you know and trust than to someone you don't know or trust.

When your project hits a rock, good ideas to overcome it can come from anywhere. Speak up, listen, respect each other, and learn.

Embrace Diversity

Every one of us has a different perspective on project issues and a different perspective on what to do about resolving those issues. The value of diversity is easy to comprehend and difficult to live. Why? Most often we assume that if we work for the same company or are in the same profession, we are similar. A team with a diversity of team members can only reap the benefits of diversity by taking time for team members to learn about their similarities and differences as to preferences for how to communicate, relate to authority, make decisions, or take or not take initiative.

A diverse project team will encounter difficulties if a clique of team members begins to think there is a right and a wrong way to being a team member. This thinking leads to certain team members viewing themselves as an in-group within the larger project team and everyone else in the out-group. In-group members know what is right and don't hesitate to criticize others not in the in-group. For a diverse team to discover its own identity, taking time to relate and communicate will reduce contentious debates and ease the pathway to finding truly innovative and effective solutions.

Manage Conflict

The silk triangle—communicate, relate, debate—is an easy way to remember that all projects are a social activity. No member of a successful project team works in a vacuum. The reason organizations are promoting and embracing diversity is because different perspectives on how to look at projects, brainstorm options, and resolve problems makes good business sense, plus it has a positive effect on the bottom line. Diversity can also mean conflict—which is valuable when engaged in competently and constructively! Conflict is scary because it can go off track and devolve into personal attacks or can end with a power play. Managing conflict competently is a key for a project's success. Learning how to do that is a challenge each team faces. Teams with great communication soon discover not everyone thinks alike, and that is a good thing!

When conflict is not about winning or losing, it is constructive. It is about being transparent and listening with respect to others' perspectives. It requires the capacity to realize everyone has a different perspective and an openness to listen to that perspective. This increases the likelihood everyone is on the same page (*communicate*), working to appreciate and respect the people expressing their ideas (*relate*) and hearing each other and have a way to argue, disagree, and eventually resolve difficult issues without harboring resentments or planning revenge (*debate*).

Decisions

> In any moment of decision, the best thing you can do is the right thing, the next best thing is the wrong thing, and the worst thing you can do is nothing.
>
> —Theodore Roosevelt

Conflict within project teams is usually resolved with a decision. There is a proper time and situation for each type of decision—unilateral, consensus, majority rule, committee, or others. Do you understand what type to use and when? Some decisions are yours to make, other decisions need team members involved, and others need to come from outside the team. Inherent to all decisions is that the decision maker never has all the information; whatever information he or she does have quickly becomes obsolete; and if a decision maker is presented with too many "good" options, he or she may experience decision paralysis. Knowing when a decision requires deliberation and when speed is required could be more important than making a wrong decision. In the story, Alex recognized the difference and chose to make a time is of the essence decision.

Speed

Meetings, reports, updating charts and logs, managing suggestions and ideas ... Taken to excess, your project time can be consumed in meetings rather than problem solving and doing. Your project can bog down with paralysis by analysis if you are not careful. At the other extreme, if one ignores these management and communication tools, then the team becomes confused and time is lost fixing mistakes created by poor communication and limited participation. Find the proper balance for your project.

Your sponsor, company, and project manager may have a high or low appetite for taking risk. This also can influence the decision process, with a direct impact on the speed with which your project progresses.

Risk

In our experience, we have yet to see a project go exactly to plan. They all have their own "rocks" waiting to be discovered. Recognizing and planning for those surprises is critical to ensuring your success. A risk register like the one in our story can itemize and prioritize risk in a way that everyone can follow and manage. A risk register is a reality check that things could go wrong and if they do, mitigate them.

Managing risk is one of the more stressful and as a result we think most avoided efforts in a project. Yet hitting the rock in your project will become even more stressful without a risk plan. You need to do a risk plan for yourself and for your project. Some of your efforts will fail and not go as expected—but that doesn't mean your project has to fail.

Attitude

Projects can be long and tiring. There will be surprises, conflict, and challenges. Learn to celebrate milestones along the way, warmly welcome new participants, and take the time to say goodbye and recognize the contributions of those who leave as the project transitions through various parts of the organization. In our story, the completion of the fence was celebrated with a party. What will be your type of celebration? Take time to laugh, enjoy each other's company, and learn new things. A positive attitude is the key to success when coupled with the confidence that the plan being followed is realistic.

To Summarize

Communicate. When you communicate well, you will discover original thoughts and opinions. But that means you need to embrace ...

Diversity. It improves performance. But diversity creates ...

Conflict. Manage conflict with respect and resolve it with good ...

Decisions. Understand who's in charge and your decision process because decisions need to occur in a timely manner, often with insufficient information, which causes ...

Risk. Face the fact every project has risks and won't go exactly to plan. But you can be successful when the team has the right ...

Attitude. Support each other, deal with surprises in a positive way, properly use project management tools, and you will discover a team that knows how to ...

Communicate again and ...

Attitude   Communicate

Risk   Diversity

Decisions   Conflict

If your project is inadequate in one or several of these six areas, it is a good indicator that your project is in trouble. If one link in the circle above becomes broken, then the whole circle eventually falls apart. Repair that broken link. You as a project team member can make the difference to keep communications open and relationships healthy, and in the process improve your own experience and discover how much it improves your project team's performance to drive the project's success.

PART IV

WHAT ABOUT AGILE?

We want to take a moment to discuss Agile. Agile methodology is increasingly popular and is an excellent method for certain projects or subsections within larger projects. Originating as a better method for software development, it has found use in some non-software applications. The easiest way to understand Agile is to review our iron triangle.

The Iron Triangle

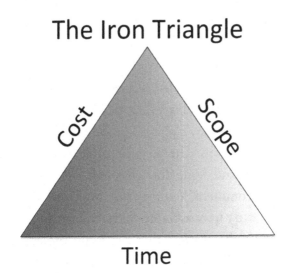

Cost

Scope

Time

Often projects are fixed in their scope. Examples include capital equipment projects, military development projects, and municipal projects. Scope-specific projects are often in the format of a contract with one customer. A specific set of deliverables must be delivered and can't be changed. We don't change the design of our bridge halfway across the river. Any "rocks" discovered in the project often increase the time and cost legs of our triangle.

Agile projects are most often fixed in time, letting cost and scope become flexible if "rocks" are discovered. Agile projects often work well for products sold into markets. A good Agile project example might be the next model of a smartphone. We don't know what features will be released with the next version (the scope is flexing as features are added and deleted and bugs fixed before release) but we do know it will be hitting the store shelves just before the holiday shopping season; it won't be late.

One key secret for Agile's success can be applied to your project regardless of the project methodology employed by your company. That secret is excellent communication, as we introduced in chapter 1. Agile employs frequent and fast team standup meetings called scrums. The team gets together for ten or fifteen minutes every day to discuss yesterday's accomplishments, today's plans, and any obstacles to success. As we've said before, the key to project success is good communication and Agile does that well.

One more comment. You may run into people who think an Agile project can't have a Gantt chart. This misunderstanding rises from the observation that an Agile project often has tasks run in parallel rather than sequentially. Sequential task planning is often called "waterfall" planning (the tasks on a

Gantt chart look like waterfall steps feeding into each other and dropping down the timeline). Remember chapter 1: All projects must have a beginning, a middle, and an end, so in reality all Agile projects can be represented by a Gantt chart and all Agile projects have sequential steps—just some of them are blended into scrums. Every Agile project has some of the sequenced steps found in any waterfall project—budget approval, stop for customer or regulatory approvals, or pre-release market testing. Those sequential steps remain; just do your best to reduce them in Agile.

This book isn't intended to be a primer on Agile methodology, but let us say it is very effective for certain projects and continues to find good applications beyond its original software-development roots.

A FINAL NOTE

We trust this story about a fence-building project and discussion about the fundamentals of project management have made you aware about how all projects, regardless of scope, are similar to the project you are currently are working on or one you have worked.

This book was written to open a doorway into the vast and complex profession of project management in such a way that you could understand basic project management methods and approaches to more effectively engage in and contribute to the projects you work on.

A short list of additional books about the topics can be found in the back of this book. You can find thousands more in bookstores or online.

BOOKS TO CONSIDER

If you wish to dig a bit more into the world of project management, there are thousands of excellent books to discover. Here are a few that might want to consider for learning more about the topics we covered.

Agile Project Management QuickStart Guide: A Simplified Beginners Guide to Agile Project Management by Ed Stark provides an introduction into this increasingly popular methodology. Agile originally was a software-development method, but its use is growing into other technical areas. Project managers debate what kind of projects are good Agile candidates; you might want to learn about Agile to provide your insight to that debate.

Becoming a CONFLICT COMPETENT LEADER—How You and Your Organization Can Manage Conflict Effectively by Craig E. Runde & Tim A Flanagan examines how dealing with conflict is difficult and provides ways to implement constructive approaches to conflict for managers and employees.

Conflict Across Cultures—A Unique Experience of Bridging Differences, by Michelle LeBaron and Venashri Pillay, gives sound guidance on how to understand general orientations influenced by culture. It provides practical ways to develop cultural fluency, how to bridge cultural divides, and ways to lessen the impact when cultures meet in the middle. For teams, this book discusses and provides real-life examples about resolving conflict that arises in culturally diverse teams.

Diversity Matters by Vivian Hunt, Dennis Layton, and Sara Prince is a publication of McKinsey & Company that provides the research to show that companies that embrace racial/ethnic diversity are 30 percent more likely to have financial results above their national industry median.

Five Dysfunctions of a Team by Patrick Lencioni describes the many pitfalls a team faces as they seek to "row together." Not a project management book per se; it addresses teamwork challenges that we find are so often the source of project troubles.

How NASA Builds Teams by Charles J. Pellerin explores an interesting discovery NASA made after several project failures. Though project failures are often due to technical issues, the root cause is most likely human error or miscommunication. Very simple and powerful methods are presented for avoiding those failures.

Intercultural Communication in the Global Workplace, by Iris Varner and Linda Beamer takes an inside look at the mechanics of intercultural communication and how the dynamics of intercultural communications play out in verbal, nonverbal, and written communications. It also describes in what are the essentials that are required for becoming culturally competent to achieve success in negotiating and resolving conflict with people from different cultures.

Nonviolent Communication a Language for Life, third editions by Marshall Rosenberg is recognized worldwide as a process for communicating observations and not judgments, expressing feelings by taking ownership of them, and knowing the difference between what you need and what you want so your want becomes a request. This book is a practical guide for how to transform your communications from tragic expressions of unmet needs into meeting needs that are life enhancing

Political Savvy—Systematic Approaches to Leadership Behind the Scenes by Joel R. DeLuca, PhD, makes the argument that being politically savvy in the workplace is not about "politics." It is about knowing how to build a critical mass of support for an idea you care about for the benefit of your team or organization. DeLuca talks about political styles, blind spots, territories, and strategies. His ethical approach to political savvy includes ways to build momentum for an idea, handling power players, and recognizing and avoiding the 101 ways to shoot oneself in the foot by knowing the organization's culture.

PRINCE2 for Dummies by Nick Graham is an excellent introduction to PRINCE2 methodology. More commonly employed in Europe but also found in North America and the rest of the world, PRINCE2 provides a nicely structured approach to project management with an emphasis on keeping that structure appropriate to each project … cover what is needed but avoid unnecessary bureaucracy.

Projects in Less Time, A Synopsis of Critical Chain by Mark J. Woeppel provides a nice summary of Eli Goldratt's Critical Chain method of project management. Critical Chain focuses on the critical path; anyone working on the critical path must stay focused and not multitask. Energies are focused to complete critical path tasks early and build a buffer to absorb the inevitable surprises ahead.

Project Management Body of Knowledge (PMBOK) is the

textbook for certification testing by the Project Management Institute. It is dry reading but is a handy reference book to provide helpful details on the topics covered in this book. If you and your teammates are struggling to determine or understand some of the ideas presented here or wish to understand them in more detail, the PMBOK can help.

Who Will Do What by When? How to Improve Performance, Accountability and Trust with Integrity by Tom Hanson, PhD, and Brigit Zacher Hanson, MS, is a must for every project team manager and member. By telling the story a formerly successful salesperson who is now a failing manager, the Hansons reveal how individuals who do what they say they will do establish personal integrity that translates into trust.

Check your local bookstore or web retailer for additional copies of this book. We also provide a companion lecture to this book that has been well received with academic and corporate teams.

ABOUT THE AUTHORS

Richard Champney, PMP, earned an engineering degree from the University of Vermont. He has extensive experience as an engineering and program manager in commercial, industrial, and military business environments. He has managed and led projects ranging from venture capital funded startups to multimillion-dollar projects. He has been a university and corporate guest lecturer on project and engineering management.

Robert W. Kubacki, J.D., M.P.A., earned a juris doctor, master in public administration, and bachelor of arts degree. His project management experience began with designing the plans to meet a nonprofit's grant deliverables and has evolved into managing numerous types of projects. He has taught courses in management, conflict resolution, and communication studies at universities in Boston and Worcester, Massachusetts, and Pittsburgh, Pennsylvania.

INDEX